MW01251220

SOAP OPERA
ACTING

The Ins and Outs of Daytime Drama

Bonnie Forward

Foreword by Lee Phillip Bell

"The only thing worse than a missed opportunity is not being ready when one comes along."

~Bonnie Forward

Dedication

To my daughter, Jordan.

You have been right by my side throughout
this rollercoaster of a Soap Opera we call Life.
I could never have done it without you. You are
the best thing that ever happened to me, my finest
accomplishment, and I love you like no other,
my beauty.

~Mama

TABLE OF CONTENTS

Foreword

I read this book and was very impressed with the knowledge and instructions about how to break into, and prepare for, daily television shows. *Soap Opera Acting - The Ins and Outs of Daytime Drama*, is an invaluable resource guide; for any actor hoping to work in Soaps, any professional wanting to succeed in the industry, Daytime historians, and, most importantly, the devoted Soap Opera fan. It is the perfect guide for anyone wanting to work in our industry. Bonnie's book is concise and gives you every opportunity to learn about the realities of working in Daytime Drama. It is hard work to be a star, but Bonnie shows you how!

Enjoy the read,

Lee Phillip Bell

Lee Phillip Bell

Co-creator, *The Young and the Restless* and *The Bold and the Beautiful*

Acknowledgments

I would like to thank, in order, the people who helped make this book happen:

To Mary Cheek, for introducing me to the world of Soap Operas where I was able to experience watching them daily for the first time in my life, thank you for starting me on the path of what would become my life's work. Rudy Vejar, who taught me everything I know about the wonderful world of Soap Operas, and whose directorial instructions in front of and behind the camera taught me how to act in, and direct, my chosen professional path, I thank you forever. Daniel Wayne Fritz, you stood by me unfailingly, made me laugh and see the fun in Soaps, and you told me to always follow my Truth. I am forever blessed that you gave me wings to keep following this adventure, with a sense of humor. Nathan Purdee, who showed me, more than anyone, the discipline necessary to act in "the best gig in town," endlessly letting me invite myself down to the set, and without whose help and support I would never have been able to continue on this amazing road.

To Lee Phillip Bell, for your amazing grace, kindness, wisdom, generosity, and unending willingness to listen to me, and to advise me whenever I needed help, I am eternally grateful to you. Your patience, guidance, constant loyalty, support, and love walked me down my life's path, my dear friend.

Last, but certainly not least, to all Soap Operas all over the globe, I thank you from the bottom of my heart for each and every daily episode of your wonderful shows, for it is watching them every day that has kept me on this incredibly brilliant professional Soap Opera journey.

FURTHER ACKNOWLEDGMENTS

I want to say a huge thank you to the following people for their contributions to this book...without each and every one of you, it would never have come to fruition.

Anita Wilson, you are my favorite wordsmith, grammarian, and forever "fiend"; Bette Beaton, your wisdom, friendship, and support guide me every day; Eva Basler, thank you for your constant love and light; Randy Graham, you got me launched, my new friend; Rich Feldman, techno genius to the stars, your computer translations were pivotal; Julie Simpson, your brutally honest, red proofreading pen lies bleeding; and Dick Orton, your visual skills are the best, my old pal, your designing expertise was critical to the look and feel of this book, and I am eternally grateful.

I love you all.

INTRODUCTION

I am a third generation Californian, born and raised in the Brentwood section of Los Angeles into an entertainment family in the 1950s. Even though my father worked in both radio and television, no televisions were ever turned on in the main parts of the house during the daytime, but they were constantly on at night because Dad worked in Primetime. We had televisions in every room, however, and our Mexican maid, Isabel, never missed watching her favorite Telenovelas during the day. I was just a small child, but I loved it! I attended a private girls' high school in Los Angeles, where one of my classes each year was Spanish. When I got home in the afternoon, Isabel would be in the middle of watching her Telenovelas and I found watching them with her was a great addition to my Spanish comprehension. You can say that Telenovelas were a huge help in my becoming a lover of languages. I was a really good writer in school; I took to it naturally, and that was instrumental in my decision to major in English Literature when I got to U.C.L.A.

I was first exposed to Soap Operas in the very beginning of the 1980s while I was staying with a friend in the Midwest. She watched them religiously, all day long. From the moment I began to watch them, I was hooked, too. I grew up on sound stages my entire young life, I had been surrounded by television and film stars on-set and off, but this style of acting was different, something I had never seen before. I was fascinated. When I returned to my home in Los Angeles, I decided to study everything I possibly could about Soap Opera Acting. I wanted to learn all there was to learn about this medium, inside and out. I studied with the best in the business. This, in turn, led to meeting many of the stars of Daytime, spending countless days on Soap sets in Hollywood, and making connections at the "top." I learned all about this business, both in front of the camera and behind the scenes, the ins and the outs, the highs and the lows, the grit and the glamour. It was then that I decided to make it my life's work to teach Soap Opera acting. I was given real scripts from top-rated Soaps to work with, and with them I began teaching workshops, classes, and giving private instruction. I have always made it a point to teach my students that, make no mistake about it, acting is 90% business and 10% show, and never is this truer than in Daytime. It is demanding, to say the least. The preparations, expectations, and qualifications needed if one is to have the absolute best chance to get an audition, land a role, and keep it, are rigorous.

Actors are always looking for ways to outdo their competition and be the best prepared in advance for a role. I know first-hand what it takes to work and succeed on a Soap. I know the people and I know this industry. I saw a growing need for a book on this subject matter, so I took my two-plus decades in this business as a Soap Opera acting coach, and I turned it into written form. It is my sincerest hope that anybody wanting to learn all about the Soap Opera genre will find this book a great resource and enjoy having a complete and comprehensive guide to this very special acting medium.

Bonnie Forward

CHAPTER ONE
Soap Operas, Serials, Novelas, Daytime Dramas

Soap Operas began on radio and the advertisers who sponsored the shows sold soap (from bathroom bar to powdered laundry) to their audience. The term "Soap Opera" was coined by the American press in the 1930s.

Serials were not called "Serials" because they aired once a week, but because they aired multiple times per week and were stories linked by narrative installments called episodes. The big difference was that you had to know what had happened in the previous installment in a serial narrative. Novelas, the Spanish word for "novels," did not mean that they were books in translation, but because they aired like you would read a novel with a continuous storyline. However, in Latin America Novelas are called a "closed" form of Soap Opera because the narrative is designed to eventually end. It is also interesting to note that Novelas dominate Primetime programming, which gives them another fundamental difference from Soap Operas in the rest of the world, which are "open" ended and only air during the day.

Daytime Drama has also become, over many decades, an accepted title for all of the above. Whatever the name, Soap Operas, Serials, Novelas, or Daytime Dramas, they all mean the same thing: a specific time when we can set aside our daily stresses and strains and tune in to escape to a place which takes us into the ongoing saga and continuing world of the daily lives of fantasy people. Everything that goes on in the characters' lives in the cities they live in, as we peek into their ups and downs, struggles and strifes, their most intimate and private moments, as their stories go on day after day, cannot help but captivate us.

Before the dawn of television, in the days of "radio only," everyone was glued to their radios at home when they weren't out "at the pictures."

Radio was the only direct link to all that was current: news, sports, music, politics, and entertainment.

Radio provided the only home entertainment via the various shows that were broadcast daily and weekly. Back in the pre-television era of radio broadcasting is when Soap Operas first debuted. It was during the 1930s, and the dark days of The Great Depression, when radio Soap Operas established themselves as the first genre of radio show to specifically target a female audience. Soaps were written as approximately 15-minute daily shows. Soap Operas such as *Painted Dreams, Woman in White, The Stolen Husband, Ma Perkins, Stella Dallas*, and dozens more, allowed millions of American women to temporarily escape the harsh social realities and economic struggles of the era. The goal of these shows was to draw in audiences, keep them captivated, and listening.

Procter and Gamble, Lever Brothers, Colgate-Palmolive, and Pillsbury were among some of the advertisers/sponsors for Soap Operas. Most network Soap Operas were produced by advertising agencies, and some were owned by the clients who sponsored them. As a result, advertisers sold a critical amount of soap products when Soap Operas aired. By 1937, Soap Operas dominated daytime radio, and in 1940 Proctor and Gamble clearly recognized what a crucial network strategy this was, and subsequently founded their own Soap Opera production company. By 1941, Soap Operas were so popular that they comprised nine out of every ten network-sponsored radio programs... 90% of the listening audience. By 1948, Daytime's ten highest-rated shows were all Soap Operas, and for advertisers that meant maintaining product recognition, and that equaled sales! Soap Opera viewers are among the most loyal, and advertisers and broadcasters recognized this. Therefore, to this day, what advertisers can sell during an episode determines the success and the life of that show.

By the 1950s, the thirty-minute Soap Opera had evolved from the fifteen-minute one. Soap Operas like *The Edge of Night, The Brighter Day, Guiding Light,* and *The Secret Storm* aired during the day, at the same time every day, five days a week, and they provided a wonderful escape for the "stay-at-home" audience, whether they were moms, dads, grandparents, aunts, uncles, brothers, sisters, housekeepers, the infirm —or maybe even you! Soap Operas were the trusted friends who were there for you every day. Products sold, and they were selling daily too! It was very clear that Soap Operas were here to stay!

Soap Operas always provided that safe, secure, and dependable place to tune in and become lost in a storyline five days a week and they still do today. With the advent of VCRs, TiVo, DVRs, Cable and the Internet, students, physicians, lawyers, accountants, everybody can now watch their favorite Soaps, bringing a whole new viewing audience to Daytime television. A *San Francisco Chronicle* reader once titled it, "55 minutes of total bliss." Geraldo Rivera, a television journalist and one-time Daytime Talk Show host had this to say about Daytime viewership: "The Daytime audience has intelligence, sensibility and a world view other than 'just' a housewife."

It's pretty incredible that the style of Daytime Drama created before the advent of television is still very much alive, and has become a cultural and media mainstay in our society. Since the dawn of that wonderful invention called television, we have now the added bonus of being able to watch the shows. It is interesting to note that *The Brighter Day*, which had an explicitly religious storyline, would move to television in 1954. However, it would be the enormously popular *Guiding Light,* with its small town characters, storylines, and plots, which would set the gold standard for all future Daytime Dramas in television. *Guiding Light* successfully moved from radio to TV on the 30th of June 1952. With these expanded plots, storylines, and additional characters, sponsors such as Colgate-Palmolive now had greater opportunity to tie-in and promote their products. While historically Soap Operas have been defined and marginalized as the genre for the "working class housewife," what has not been acknowledged is that Soaps have incorporated some of the most complex and sophisticated storylines while also utilizing most of the important developments in mass media.

In addition, Soaps were also at the forefront of exploring and reflecting cultural and taboo social issues, such as: infidelity, divorce, illegitimacy, blackmail, political scandal, domestic violence, drug and alcohol addiction, murder, amnesia, civil rights, women's rights, abortion, homosexuality, long lost loves, teenage pregnancy, interracial marriage, AIDS, and single parenthood. In fact, it is difficult to think of a social or political issue which has not been explored and developed through Daytime storylines. The writers have worked so tirelessly and creatively to bring such issues to life day after day through the lives of their characters. This requires an extremely receptive and intelligent audience, who is willing and capable of sustaining a high level of understanding on multiple levels and is not just watching for "low brow" escapism.

Remarkably, Daytime Drama never skipped a beat during the transition from radio to television. First, we saw Soap Operas in black and white when television first became popular, and now in "living" color. Essential to any Soap Opera is continuity and now there was much more room to expand. The freedom that came with shows now being on-camera was wonderful! The storylines retained their same melodramatic tone and flavor, but now they were expanded in so many new and exciting ways. This gave birth to being able to add many more cast members to the shows, which in turn enabled the writers to breathe much more life and detail into the characters' lives. In both old and new Soaps, greater depth, layer, and texture could be woven into the storylines. Characters could now be explored in new ways with rich and in-depth characterizations. Daytime TV was here to stay and Soap Opera fans were mesmerized.

Daytime television is a cash cow and, as an actor, staying on a Soap is dependent entirely on how the ratings fare, and how well the sponsors' products sell on that network in that time slot. It's all about advertising dollars. All of that is contingent upon how much your viewing audience relates to your particular portrayal of your character, which in turn determines how much your portrayal of your character makes them want to watch your storyline. Keeping your audience faithful every day, five days a week, has always meant, and still means, product sales first and foremost. Sales is what keeps your show alive. Sales of product in Daytime Television is what also keeps Primetime TV alive. Most of you didn't know that, did you? Advertising and product placement is everything. It has been true since the days that Soaps first began on radio.

In order to keep your "Serial" continuously popular producers had to sell products. In the days of radio everything was based on keeping your listening audience captivated and that meant *sound*. From that day to this nothing has changed in that regard; however, with the addition of the visual component of TV, you also have to look good. It wasn't easy for actors to make the transition from radio to TV, and often a great voice did not necessarily mean an actor had good looks too. A fair number of radio talent did not possess both, so those who couldn't make the visual transition to TV stayed in radio. Thus was ushered in a new form of auditioning; the search for that perfect, winning combination of sight and sound, good looks and a great voice.

The impact of the phenomenal success of Daytime serialization was not lost on the corporate sponsors, network executives, and rapidly expanding generational fan base. It was no longer "just" housewives who were watching Soaps. Inevitably, this cultural and social shift was noted by Primetime TV executives and advertising agencies. By the 1970s, the success of Daytime serialization was a given. Now network advertisers began to vie for a share of this extremely lucrative and loyal market. The hidden reality is that Daytime Drama advertising monies have always paid for Primetime television. For their Primetime productions, the density of product advertising and sales on Daytime television created a financial windfall and foundation for networks across the board.

The audience, who had grown up with Daytime Drama, now looked to Primetime for the same level of action, melodrama, suspense, and sophistication in their evening viewing. It is no coincidence that such Primetime hits as *Dallas, Dynasty, Knots Landing, Falcon Crest, ER, St. Elsewhere, LA Law*, had all become the inheritors of the Daytime television formula, and in turn went on to create their own generational legacy of serialization.

By 1976, *TIME* magazine would write that daytime television was "TV's richest market." And everything in this market was now open to development, branding, and product placement by and for the mainstream audience. Music, fashion, interior design, and hairstyles were all embraced and consumed with fervor by the mainstream viewers.

Even with the significant social impact and loyal fan base of Daytime Soaps, the scales were beginning to tip in favor of Primetime, Cable, and Internet dramas. Still, the willingness and commitment of Soaps to remain relevant on social issues, the growing diversity in the casting of characters, and the ever-present and evolving romantic storylines allowed for Soaps to remain at the forefront, and also created an entirely new fan base.

Daytime producers desired to make their Soaps more accessible to all of their loyal fans by strategically utilizing the new media of the exploding market share of the Internet and Cable. Soaps began to use media such as YouTube, AOL video, SOAPnet.com, SoapCentral, Crackle.com, and soaps.com. In addition, the unprecedented popularity of the new social networking world and pop culture-driven media such as Facebook, Twitter, and Soap blogs appealed to an entirely new, younger, and media savvy demographic fan base. Now, all Soap fans of any age, elementary school-aged kids to the hip and fun senior citizens set, could stay current with their favorite characters, evolving storylines, and the complex and sometimes convoluted romantic liaisons of their Soaps. Through the tools of the new media, fans are now able to watch teasers and previews, enjoy interviews with their favorite Daytime stars, and most importantly view recaps of any missed episodes. Beyond broadening the age demographic of their fan base, the new media has also allowed Soaps to reach a new global audience. Now, American Soaps are being broadcast all over the world, sometimes twice a day!

There is no getting around it, it is the timelessness and social relevancy of Daytime Drama storylines of love, loss, jealousy, and revenge which transcend the cultural and social barriers of geography and history.

CHAPTER TWO
Getting Started

You have decided you want to be a Soap Opera actor. The first thing to establish is which show(s) you wish to be cast on. After you make that decision, you needed to know where the studio is located: East Coast or West Coast. The general question has always been, is it produced in New York or Los Angeles? Things have been changing over the years, most Soaps are now shot exclusively in Los Angeles, so it may not be as simple as determining which Coast you will live on.

Next, you need to read the latest entertainment opportunities in a "complete online Actors Resource" like *Back Stage West, The Working Actors Guide*, and any and all other casting-related trade magazines. Read them all from front to back, also go online and read everything you can find. In all of these resources you will find everything about Film, TV, Cable, Theater, and Commercial Production that is going on around town. This is important information and you will need to know all of it. It is called knowing your craft. It is essential if you want to work in this business. It is just like studying for any other job. You must be thorough! In addition, acting coaches, photographers, dance classes, hair and make-up artists, and other industry professionals all advertise in these various trade sources. Call around, ask questions, and don't be shy, networking is part of the job.

CHAPTER THREE
Acting Classes

I have been an Acting Coach for more than 25 years. I have taught acting for commercials, daytime television, primetime television, cable television, theater, and film to children, teens, and adults. The world of acting is an extremely competitive business, and there is no substitute for being prepared and taking acting classes. It is the most essential ingredient in the process of preparation to work in this field. Many "wannabe" Soap Opera actors think they can just skip the studying process by jumping ahead and paying to attend Casting Director Workshops and Seminars, Agent Workshops and Seminars, and other types of industry venues. I am telling you these forums are for experienced actors, who know something about the business of acting—not for newcomers and beginners. You will be wasting precious time and money, and since you need to hand out your headshot and resume to them, they will remember you.

Every headshot ends up in a file somewhere after you attend these events. Listen when I tell you to take every acting class you can find. Study everything from Improvisation to Commercials to Scene Study to Soap Opera to Theater to Film and every television class in between. Study, study, study! Plus, it looks good on your resume. Casting Directors are always interested in who you are studying with, because it tells them you are keeping up your "chops" and staying fresh. It is often one of the first questions they will ask you: "Who are you currently studying with?"

There are A LOT of acting coaches out there teaching classes and an equal number of "styles" of instruction, so try and audit a class before you sign up to take one. Any good acting coach worth studying with will allow this; I always have. Do NOT, however, become a "professional acting class auditor"! Nothing is more "un" professional than someone who wants to be an actor, but who doesn't want to pay to take complete class courses to achieve that goal. Remember, THERE ARE NO SHORTCUTS.

An acting class is a cohesive group that gathers to work together much like an ensemble cast. Every week you get different scene partners and you rehearse, rehearse, rehearse for the next week so that you can be off-book when you come to class. My classes teach cold reading technique as well as rehearsed material, because I know and understand the importance of learning both. You cannot get on a Soap or any other acting job if you cannot cold read, because many auditions are cold readings. You must learn how to memorize copious dialogue to stay employed as a Soap actor. I didn't use a camera when I began teaching acting 25 years ago, because I was teaching so many types of acting; however, when I decided to specialize in Soap Opera, every class became an on-camera one. I always have my actors work from all original scripts from two of the top rated Soap Operas in every class. I find it invaluable to see yourself on camera and that is how I learned when I studied with the 4-time Daytime Emmy Award-winning director for *The Young and the Restless*, Rudy Vejar. It is a reality check the first time you see and hear yourself on camera. My first-time actors are always hilarious with their comments.

Most evenings, my first time students will say: "That's ME???", "I had NO idea I sounded like that!", "I look so weird!!"

Every acting coach is as different as the students they teach, and each one has a style all their own, so it is important to find the ones that you know will challenge you. I have a saying in my classes: "Leggo your ego at the door." And nothing is more important to remember when you start any acting class. You want an acting coach who is going to bring out the best in you as an actor in a performance. Try to take one class at least once a week or more if possible. You can focus on one class at a time or mix them up to where you are taking several types of classes every week. It's just like exercise of any kind; you are preparing to work in a highly competitive business, so in order to stay in shape you have to work to your potential and stretch yourself. While you are taking classes, also think about getting cast in a local theater production. There are always plenty of them around, and it is fabulous preparation for being on a Soap. It teaches you to build that fourth wall and to work with an ensemble cast. Acting in plays can be a critical component of your starting out, because you begin expand your repertoire of work and fill up your resume. It is an invaluable acting experience and Casting Directors make a point to get out and see actors in local theater productions. Also send invitations to any plays you are performing in to the Casting Directors you are targeting, and not just once, but every week of the play's run. It is a wonderful way to get ahead of the pack! Even after you land your job on a Soap, continue studying. It keeps you fresh.

CHAPTER FOUR

Headshots

Before you see a Casting Director, you must have headshots taken by a good photographer. When you begin looking for a professional headshot photographer you will be calling to make an appointment to see their "book." It is always a good idea to first ask if they have photographed Soap actors before. There are dozens and dozens of professional headshot photographers out there. If they haven't had the experience of tailoring their work towards actors who as a result have found work on a Soap because of that photographer's brand of work, then move on to a photographer who has worked with Soap actors. You needn't spend a great deal of money to have some really good headshots taken, either. Casting Directors couldn't care less whether you went to a super expensive "Hollywood headshot" photographer or not. A Casting Director just wants to see a good, crisp, clear picture of you and to make sure you look exactly like your headshot when you walk into their office. NO re-touching, "soft focus" shots, or anything that detracts from exactly what you look like in person.

This brings me to my next important point, which is wardrobe. I have often advised my students to wear to their audition what they wore in their headshots because it shows consistency of your look. Keep your clothing simple—no patterns, prints, layering or jewelry accessories. I advise you to look at what actors wear on your favorite shows to develop ideas regarding color, style, and appropriateness. You can submit either black and white and/or color shots. My preference is black and white, but learn what your Casting Director prefers by contacting the offices for the show and asking them. You are going to want a range of shots as well. You need to have them ready for any part you might be up for (wearing anything from edgy leather jacket to conservative business power suit), and please, NO bathing suit shots, guys and gals!

Remember, it is important to DO YOUR HOMEWORK throughout every step of this process. There are plenty of good photographers out there who can do a terrific job and who don't cost an arm and a leg. I know, I used to be married to one! It is important to interview several photographers, and to really take your time looking through their books. Their books will vary and it is important that you know what you are looking for. Go to the supermarkets, drugstores, or discount stores where they stock Soap Opera magazines and purchase a few. Then, take them home and look through them at the headshots of the actors. Study what they are wearing and how they are posing. I am not talking about the studio's photos from scenes from the shows, also known as "stock photos," but rather the obviously posed-for headshots. Take the best ones with you to show to your photographer. Now, you are ready to book your photographer. Once you decide to book with them, they will go over what clothing changes you will need to bring to the shoot, if you will want a Make-up Artist there, and whether you will want both indoor and outdoor shots. All this is extremely important and must be clearly decided upon beforehand, so take notes on what your photographer tells you. After your shoot it will take approximately two weeks to get your finished product.

You will need to go over/review the proof sheets from the shoot and decide which ones will be printed. Later, you will take those original shots, have your name put on them, and have them printed in bulk for distribution to various Casting Directors. If you have an existing acting resume that is great, but if you don't that is okay, because you will fill it up with acting classes that you have taken. Print your name and phone number(s) on quality 8x10 paper and attach it to the back of your headshot. Please make sure that the phone number you list is one that you will answer! Nothing is more aggravating to a Casting Director than trying to reach an actor who does not answer their phone promptly when it rings —or cannot be reached at all! They will simply move on to the next headshot that is on their desk, call that actor, and you will have missed your opportunity. Always remember this is a highly competitive business that you are entering, and there is only one you. However, there are thousands of actors who want to work on Soaps like you, so be prepared!

Here's your to-do list so far:

- Research a headshot photographer
- Hire and discuss details of the shoot
- Review proof sheets and choose your shots
- Organize headshots with resume
- Double-check your personal and contact information on your resume and headshots (name, address and telephone number)
- Submit to the appropriate Casting Directors

Now you are ready to get going in your quest to work on a Soap Opera!

CHAPTER FIVE
Casting Directors and the Auditioning Process

I am often asked: "If Soap Operas have a regular cast ensemble then what do the casting directors do? What purpose do they serve on a daily basis? Why are they needed?"

Well, as I mentioned earlier, soap scripts are written approximately four months in advance of production; however, there may also be many last-minute changes. A Soap Opera Casting Director's job is to work directly with the writers on a daily basis and anticipate their needs. Some actors choose to leave their Daytime jobs to pursue other acting opportunities outside of Daytime, and their parts must be either recast or an entirely new character brought in to fill the void. Casting Directors see actors daily, and keep your photos on file. And oh yes, even the bad actors' photos go into a file.

So, don't try to change your look or your name to come back and try and trick your way through another casting call! Casting Directors keep constant files for when the writers need a new character; they are ready to audition new actors or recall actors they have already auditioned. They go through their files first to see who physically matches the new or recast "look" the writers are searching for. Then, they send out the calls to see those actors they previously liked and any new ones they would like to audition for the first time. Believe me, when a cast member suddenly decides to jump ship you want your Casting Director ready to cast YOU! Sometimes, a storyline is taken in a different direction by the writers, and again, you want that Casting Director ready at a moment's notice.

When casting of a major character takes place, the Casting Director, and Assistant Casting Director, work very hard; sometimes seeing up to 40 actors' headshots a day, 25 of whom come into their offices and read the same scripts one after another, all day long. On other days they see far fewer, but they never stop auditioning actors because you never know what the writers have in mind for the next storyline. I recall an instance when I had a student who was extremely miffed when he went to audition for a very prominent Soap Opera Casting Director. Apparently, she stood up and turned her back to him and walked over to a filing cabinet while he was reading his lines. He came back to me furious that she could have been so rude... in his estimation. Well, I asked him if he had ever considered the possibility that it was deliberate. No, he hadn't, and he did not understand why I would suggest that such a thing would be deemed acceptable! I explained to him that not all people who watch soaps are glued to their sets watching every move, gesture, and word. In fact, many viewers get up and do other things with their backs to the sets. Often they are listening from another room, cleaning, cooking or doing chores. Therefore, one's performance had better have excellent listening appeal, and not just visual appeal. Remember what I mentioned earlier about how Soap Operas got their start on radio? The audience obviously couldn't see the actors, and listening was all there was, so your vocal ability to sustain and keep the attention of your listening audience was crucial in maintaining the interest of your audience, and their on-going loyalty to the show. My student suddenly "got it" and vowed to "wow" any Casting Director in the future with his voice and vocal cadence as well as his acting abilities.

If you get this far in the process, you hope for a "call back." If you appear to be a good fit and the Casting Director likes you, then you will get a call back for a second reading. The Casting Director and the Producers begin the process of separating the wheat from the chaff. It is at this point that you will most likely be put on tape. This is only your first hurdle, however, because your tape is now sent on to the writers and producers for review. After all, you have to "fit in" with an already existing cast. You must also be right as a real person, as well as the character you are being considered for. You are walking into an already existing cast "family" which has been there for a long time, and it is you that must fit in with them, and not the other way around! In this business, nobody was or is beyond replacement, ever. So, as you can see, a Casting Director's job is very necessary indeed. From the start, they can make you or they can break you.

If you are lucky enough to receive a call back, it is a good rule of thumb when you are handed your audition script to read the first page, and then skip to the last. This allows you to know exactly where your character is going, literally and figuratively. The reason behind this is so that if you do not have time to read all the pages before you are called in to "read," then at least you will know where your character is going in the scene and where you will end up. The pages in between will fall into place if you have at least had time to read the first and last pages of the scene. In a soap script it is all written out for you, including the blocking. ("Blocking" is the term used in acting to describe how an actor moves around the furniture in a scene.) Soap Opera sets are for the most part very small. How many steps you need to take to reach a certain place on the set is a key component to working with the three cameras when shooting a scene. We will cover the 3-camera shoot in a later chapter. I tell you this because sometimes you do not have your script in advance, but arrive at the studio for a general audition and are given it then and there. You can be called in without adequate time to prepare or rehearse your lines, much less know anything about your character! This is a crucial tip!

Also, don't ever give everything you've got to each of your rehearsals. Your final performance when you are in front of the Casting Director and the camera is the moment when you bring it all out. Save "it" for the camera; it makes you "in the moment" and that translates very effectively to the camera. *This is the big secret to acting in Soaps!* You have to be consistent but not over-rehearsed; save your "in the moment" for in the moment!

As I said earlier, Soap Operas are all about sex, sincerity, and authenticity, and if you cannot bring that to your first audition you will never get through. I know this seems like a lot to digest, but you have to be very aware of every step of what you are doing as you begin the process of getting through to the writers and producers! I have included a sample page of what a character description looks like. When you receive a page like this, you will know exactly who your character is, what motivates your character, why their intentions are what they are, and how they are going to exhibit behavior that is exclusive to them.

JOSH JOHNSON
(A Character Description)

Josh Johnson is a man of deep secrets, and his persona is designed to keep his secrets deeply hidden. He is tall, young (24-29) and devastatingly handsome. He is very toned, well built, and years as a farm hand have sculpted his body into a lean, strong, muscular form. Josh is a soft-spoken, quiet man of few words, but he is intense. He has no curiosity about people and volunteers nothing about himself. On the surface he appears to be a simple ordinary man who makes his living working a farm. But Josh is much more than that. He is highly intelligent and very well educated. He writes in his spare time and his writings are deep and complex and tell of deep pain and some long-hidden injustices. Josh does not anger easily, but when he is pushed he becomes fierce. He possesses a dry wit, but he only shows it to those people he trusts and is most comfortable with—there are very few. Josh can achieve anything he puts his mind to, and once he has set himself a goal he pursues it with a single-minded determination bordering on obsession. Josh has a power over women that is dynamic and it stems from a combination of his strength, sensitivity, and sensuality.

All women, young, old and in-between, cannot help but be attracted to him. Josh uses his sensual physicality carefully, although he knows he could have any woman he wants. He has taste and is discriminating when it comes to women. He has loved more than once, but no woman has ever truly captured his heart and he has never bared his soul to any of them. He then meets Pamela Edwards. Josh has come to town with a specific goal in mind and he intends to achieve it. He will not be sidetracked by anyone. But he is immediately drawn to Pamela and feels a deep connection. He feels a kinship to the pain she feels towards losing her love, Brian Moore. He sees how much pride she exhibits in the face of her heartbreak. In spite of himself, Josh cannot help but reach out to Pamela. Is he motivated by her youth, beauty, and irresistibility? Or could this be the first woman to finally unlock the secrets of Josh's soul?

CHAPTER SIX
Agent, Manager, or Entertainment Attorney?

I have always advised my students that your next step should be to visit the Academy of Motion Picture Arts and Sciences library. It has catalogues of Actors, Managers, and Agents. These are enormous books that list representatives of individual actors. This is to ensure that you do not seek out a representative who has another actor who looks just like, or very similar to, you in their "stable," as it is known in the business. Always remember this is a business first and a show second. As mentioned, it is 90% business and 10% show. Never burn any bridges in this business. This does not mean you become anyone's doormat or put up with being ill-treated or discriminated against; however, it is important that you address any concerns and grievances professionally and courteously through the appropriate channels. This is not advice you will likely receive from someone who is going to represent you.

Some actors are hired as "day players," but soon find that because the fans like them so much, or the writers decide to expand the storyline, they are now bumped up to Contract status. When you are handed your first contract and you don't already have an agent or manager, you need to decide whether you want one, both, or are just as happy hiring only an entertainment attorney to negotiate your contract for you. It is very important and critical to realize that contracts are negotiated once when you are hired, and later when they are up for renewal.

Contracts on Soaps, to start with, are 13 days in 13 weeks guaranteed. Then you are moved up to 26 days in 26 weeks, then 52 days in 52 weeks. It doesn't matter if you get a 3-year contract or a 5-year contract; the producers always reserve the right to terminate you at the end of ANY of those contractual time periods. Whether you are doing hospital scenes where you barely speak, because you have been poisoned by a toxic martini from a vengeful lover, become comatose because you have been run over by your jealous step-daughter, suddenly rendered mute due to a viral brain infection, or you have been given a fabulous front burner storyline with significant dialogue, your pay is the same as has been negotiated.

As far as agents' and managers' percentages and attorneys' fees are concerned, do your homework. Talk to everyone in the industry who is willing to speak with you, ask about fees, and check around.

CHAPTER SEVEN
Acting in Daytime

"Two rules of thumb on a Soap Opera: Never turn your back to the camera and never look straight into it." ~Rudy Vejar, four-time consecutive Emmy Award-Winning Director for *The Young and the Restless*

Today, Daytime Drama remains for the actor the closest thing we still have to the old Hollywood studio system. Essentially, the show owns you, they protect you, and they take care of you. Everything to do with you as a cast member is handled by the show. It is very similar to when an actor was signed on in the past as a contract player at a major Hollywood motion picture studio such as MGM, Columbia, RKO, Paramount, Fox, or Warner Bros. Back then, the studio took complete care of their actors. Everything from press publicity (many times with very carefully planted stories) to what doctor treated you, to your dance classes, wardrobe, and make-up — all was arranged for and taken care of by the studio you were under contract to. It was a society within its own world, and with its own norms, standards, loyalties, hierarchies, and taboos.

It is a wonderfully secure feeling to have everything looked after for you by your studio. For the right actor looking for job security, there is nothing better than a job on a Soap Opera. Should you want to venture outside of the show, however, you must ask permission. Always check and read the fine print in your contract. After you've read and checked the fine print, remember that when you work on a Soap you have far more freedom, but you are still under strict contract. Avoid visions of personal grandeur and let the powers that be at your network and show do the majority of the talking for you. If you do not understand this, you will be very sorry. I have known a few actors who became very bitter with their shows, the writing team, the producers, and the network. They became so ego-driven; they didn't like the "direction" their storylines were going in, they suddenly wanted things their way, and they no longer respected what the show wanted. It is perfectly okay to go to your bosses and ask for input into your storyline, it's artistic input after all, but remember this is your job and they are your bosses. Trust them to do their jobs as they trust you to do yours. I cannot emphasize this enough. It is important to know your position within the greater scheme of things, because if you don't want this job, ah well, there are thousands who would love to take your place. There is a very strict hierarchy in show business. If you are someone who wants to be steadily employed as a television actor, and this type of system does not appeal to you, please read no further. These are the rules and they are never going to change.

You have to be smart to act on a Soap Opera. You have to read extremely well, be articulate, intelligent, and have a great memory. I don't care how good-looking you are, if you don't have the "smarts" to back up those looks, you will never make it onto a Soap.

It is a combination of looks and intelligence that will land you the role and keep you on the show. Working on a Soap is very hard work, and it takes a very special actor indeed to be able to do it. Yes, there are occasional "character actor" parts, but they are rare. I have known many famous Soap Opera actors, but I have never known a single one who was both successful and dumb. It takes a certain type of person with a certain character and disposition to be dedicated to acting in a Soap. Acting in Daytime is an extremely specific type and style of acting. It is all about re-acting, not just acting. It can be said that this is true for all forms of acting, but never as true as it is in Soap Opera. Any actor can act "out," but how well you *react* to your scene partner(s) is the key to successful acting in Soaps. The close-ups are constant, and they capture the character's innermost feelings.

When you are handed your first soap in a soap script your job is to figure out what the writers have written by analyzing the scene script, dissecting the writers' words, digesting those words, and expressing those words on camera exactly as the writers have written them, and I mean exactly. Everything is written out for you in a soap script: what to emote, when to emote, and how to emote, along with all the "blocking" instructions (i.e., when to move and where, what prop to pick up when and what to do with it), all your BEATS, your PAUSES, and all the director's instructions, such as when there is to be an Extreme Close Up (ECU) or FADE TO BLACK. If it is a Voice Over (V.O.), it is all written out on the page. BEAT written on the pages of a script means that before you deliver your line, you count four Mississippi's (1 Mississippi, 2 Mississippi, 3 Mississippi, 4 Mississippi) after you see that word BEAT. Each beat is so very important to the dramatic emphasis of the script. There is a deliberately slow pace to Soap Operas and you cannot afford to skip even one. Never forget, the writers have written their lines for you to deliver exactly as they created them, and that most definitely includes each and every beat. PAUSE means just that; it is not a BEAT.

Not only are there acting beats, but there are musical beats as well. Music is used to transition from one scene to the next. Your script often reads where the music is to be inserted. Music, in the days of radio Soaps, was an organ playing for the dramatic Friday cliffhanger, and dramatic emphasis to transitioning scenes, as I mentioned earlier. Now, in Daytime, Primetime, and Cable television it is used throughout for dramatic effect: to technically transition from one scene to another, to highlight a scene, to underscore a romantic interlude, to foreshadow a dark moment, and to add an element of poignancy. Beyond these functions, music in Soaps is used for all types of emphasis. The editors are in charge of the over-dubbing, the actors never hear the music unless it is live, and the editing work begins after that day's particular shoot is finished. Many professional musicians have contributed their popular music to Soaps, many have appeared on Soaps, and Soaps have also launched many an actor's successful musical career.

To see what an actual Soap script looks like, what follows are two sample pages:

PROLOGUE - SCENE THREE PAMELA'S MOTEL ROOM

(PAMELA AT DESK, WORKING ON A DRAWING SHE'S MADE...
WHICH IS A LAYOUT OF THE BALLROOM. SHE EXAMINES THE
DRAWING INTENTLY, TRACING DETAILS WITH HER PENCIL,
AS)

                    CATHY (V.O.)

Okay... the main circuit breaker box is there... the door
that goes in there is locked, but no problem.

(BEAT)

(BEAT)

                    CATHY (V. O.)

This plan has to be fool-proof! I need more information
about Pamela Edwards... (BEAT, AS, ALOUD TO
HERSELF)

Calm down, Cathy. It's going to be fine. There'll be
plenty of time to learn all about the lady... her habits,
her patterns, her likes and dislikes...

And then I'll get rid of her.

I'll get in there... see where Pamela Edwards is and keep an eye on her. Then, when I see her stand still... I'll hit the switch. The lights go out.

(BEAT)

It will be totally dark. I can DO this... finish her off. (BEAT) And Roy is mine.

(A COLD, UNFEELING DEMEANOR ... AS WE HOLD... THEN...)

CATHY (CONT'D)

(ANGRILY, SHE TEARS UP THE DRAWING, AS)

I'm just not ready! Damn! I need more time.

(BEAT, SHE PACES, AS, VOICE OVER)

(BEAT)

Because she can't have him. He's mine. Roy is mine!

(SHE STANDS THERE FOR A MOMENT, DETERMINED... THEN SHE SLOWLY BRINGS HERSELF DOWN... THE ANGER AND DETERMINATION SEEM TO DISSOLVE FROM HER FACE, AS A SOFTER LOOK COMES OVER HER... SHE MOVES TO HER CELLPHONE, LOOKS AT A NUMBER... AS)

25

When you read the script, ask yourself: who is doing what to whom and why? If you do not do that first, you will be lost as to how to approach your character's involvement with your fellow actors as well as the storyline. Remember, the storylines have been going on before you came along and they will continue to go on regardless of whether you stay or leave the show. I cannot emphasize enough, do your homework before you ever consider becoming a soap actor!!

Daytime Drama is not a medium for "method" actors. In fact, Soap Opera acting is the antithesis of Method Acting. Soap Operas are fast moving, in the moment, full of more dialogue than you can imagine; you have a limited number of takes (on some soaps you only get one), you are working with a number of other actors who are prepared before they get to the set (sometimes memorizing your lines as well as their own), and with directors who are on a short schedule per scene and there is no time for actors who have to "go into a corner and come out an orange"! There is a famous story about Sir Laurence Olivier and Dustin Hoffman when they were filming *Marathon Man* in New York City's Central Park. Hoffman having studied Method Acting extensively, was "getting into character" by running around the Central Park lake and he asked Olivier to join him to get into character for the scene. Olivier simply remarked something like this: "My dear boy, why don't you just try 'acting'?" I don't know whether that is a true story, but you get the message.

Soap Operas are an hour show or a half hour show, depending, and are shot in one day, completed and "in the can" that same evening. This is done five days a week, 52 weeks a year...not counting holidays. You have a copious amount of dialogue to memorize every day, although you will not always be working every day, obviously, due to the size of the cast. The more you work, the more front burner storyline you have, the more money you make, and, most importantly, remember, this is your job.

I overheard a very famous Daytime star in the studio one morning advising a young newcomer to his show. Here is what he had to say: "Soap Opera is all about dialogue, storyline, and the characters. A Soap Opera is lucky if they have two out of those three." He used the Soap Opera *Santa Barbara* to illustrate his point by going on to say, "*Santa*

Barbara had really crisp dialogue and snappy characters with snappy lines like a play has; however, they didn't have much of a storyline." The young actor asked him, "How do you memorize all of these lines every night?" and he replied, "You don't focus on memorizing the lines, you focus on the scene, you focus on what's going on in the scene. If you focus on trying to memorize all the words and the lines the night before, you are going to compromise your health, you are going to be exhausted, and it is futile to do that. Better to know what is going on in the scene, where you are going in the scene, and what's happening in the scene. Then, in the morning when you come in to do your blocking, you can go through your dialogue and do that. It's about short-term memory, not long-term. This is something that is to be digested as quickly as possible, memorized as quickly as possible, and delivered as quickly as possible, and then put out there when you are taping the scene."

I must reiterate that this is the hardest acting job you will **EVER** have. The easy part: show up prepared, say your lines, throw out your script (you will never have to look at it again, although some actors choose to keep every one of their scripts at home in a type of library), pick up your next one, and leave the studio. Of course, you are assigned a dressing room if you are a castmate, so if you have an early call time, you can always stay at the studio and work out of your dressing room anytime you like. You are also free to come into the studio early if you have an 11:00 am or noontime call time if you want to get a jump on things. I like to put the job of acting on a Soap Opera this way: "Some actors work for a while and some work for a lifetime; if you're lucky, you're a Soap actor who works for a lifetime."

CHAPTER EIGHT

Making the Final Cut/Getting Through to the Writers and Producers

Your audition tape will be seen by the writers and producers before you are, so by now you should be ready to sit down with the powers that be, audition again, and discuss your role. You will be asked to read again. Often they will bring in the actor your character will have the most storyline with to read with you. They will, among other things, be evaluating the chemistry you have with this castmate before determining your suitability for the role. You will be taped again with that actor; so that the writers and producers can review it later...after you are gone from the room.

This is the time to bring out everything you've got to give the character while also maintaining a delicate balance of not being "over the top." If you try to "top" your scene partner you will embarrass yourself and look like a selfish actor. It is the most foolish of moves an actor can make, because the show is a team effort, and as such, all actors must give and take. Always make your partner look good, is a good rule of thumb to follow. You are with the same actors day in and day out, so this is all about collaboration and how well you can give as an actor to your co-stars. It is your *job*. The writing team and producers will be watching you very carefully as you tread this delicate path. This does not diminish you as an actor, but rather enables you to be part of an ensemble cast where you will be supported, long term, unlike any other acting job. You will be able to have all the room you need to flex your acting muscles both in monologues and dialogues, as your storyline dictates, in the days, months, and years to come as you progress in your work and career. You now have an amazing opportunity to grow and stretch as an actor all within the role of one character. Of course, if they give you the marvelous experience of having an evil/good twin or playing a character with multiple personalities, all the better for you!

Chapter Nine
Landing the Role

Congratulations! You landed the role! You will immediately be required to join the union that governs you as an actor, SAG-AFTRA (The American Federation of Television and Radio Actors (AFTRA) and The Screen Actors Guild (SAG). It is called "SAG-AFTRA Must Join," and you can no longer work without joining. The union enforces this rule by requiring producers to verify the actor's status by contacting the union. If you don't pay, they will fine your paychecks until your dues are paid in full.

It is one thing to get the role, it is quite another to keep it. Your ability to remain on any show is dependent on whether or not your audience likes you, loves you, or just loves to hate you. It is all up to you now.

Sometimes you land the role you were up for only to discover suddenly that the writers have decided to create yet another character for you. They and the producers have now made the decision that you are better suited to the newer role. This has happened countless times throughout Soap Opera history, and you need to be capable of immediately switching to an entirely different character. After all, you are a full-fledged actor now, are you not? I have heard many a Soap actor note that their new role was better than the original role they auditioned for. Sometimes, the switch is made at the final cut of the role that you and someone else were both up for; the writers decided to write in a second character, interchange those characters, and give you each a role. This is not only a great opportunity, but it prepares you for all the variables your character will go through throughout the show's storylines.

Don't make the mistake of ever getting cocky or too comfortable when you get your first role. Remember, you can always be replaced and many actors often are because they just don't fit in. This is an ensemble cast you are joining and they were there before you, and whether you stay or go, they will be there after you. This is your new family and you are its newest member. Make friends, learn as much as you can, keep your mouth shut, and do your job! I remember the actor Tom Selleck, who started on Daytime when he was cast by William (Bill) J. Bell on *The Young and The Restless,* say once that he likes working best with an ensemble cast, because he isn't in every scene and he isn't expected to carry the whole show. All that is asked of you in an ensemble is that you give the show your complete loyalty, be on time, know your lines, and make those viewers love you, and for that you are paid a great deal of money. Often, you may not start off with a front-burner storyline, but that can change in the blink of an eye, if the fan mail starts coming in and/or the writers decide to up your character's involvement in a current storyline. BE PREPARED!!

True, it is not a Primetime television or film role where you have far less dialogue and you get paid much more money, but you have a steady job year round, not just for the length of a series or the length of a film. This is any actor's dream, believe me, and anyone who to tells you differently is either jealous, lying, or both. Just ask any non-working actor how they would feel about having a steady Soap Opera role.

CHAPTER TEN
The Writing Team

RESPECT THE WRITERS! There are cadres of them! Don't ever try to rewrite, improvise, or "interpret" what the writers have written. *They* have created the characters, and they have worked tirelessly on those characters and storylines. The writers are the ones who know everything about how their characters came to be, where they come from, why they do what they do, and who they are. The writers are constantly creating, recreating, and un-creating their characters. Now it is time to "own" your character. You need to study their history, who they are, what makes them tick, what their connection is to the other characters, how and why they came to be who they are, and then with this knowledge, breathe life into the character and become them.

Be aware that Soap writers write their storylines approximately four to five months in advance. Soap characters are written as very deep and complicated people, as are their storylines. Soap Opera writers' words are sacred and their storylines are never to be crossed, challenged, or changed by you. Another extremely important thing is to always remember, *regardless of your contract*, the writers created you, and they can "UN-create" you just as quickly. Always keep in mind that the writers have the power to, literally, write you off the show. So, stay on your toes. There is a *huge* difference between being let go from a Daytime Soap for creative reasons, being fired from the show, or deciding to leave the show of your own accord.

If the show lets you go, it is usually because you and your character didn't work out in terms of the projected storyline, the fan mail pouring in (or not) towards you as an actor was unfavorable, or the writers just simply changed their minds. I've seen actors who were written off of a Soap, but because of a firestorm of complaints from loyal viewers were then written back into the show. Ratings determine EVERYTHING. If nobody is watching your show, nobody is buying the products sold on it, whatever the reason.

If you are in the unfortunate position of being fired from a show, it is probably due to one of the following reasons: poor professionalism, flagrant violation of contract obligations, you caused serious discord behind the scenes, or you had simply been unable to work well within an ensemble cast. *Never* get angry about it and *never* talk about it publicly. Whatever the reasons for your termination with the show, it is important that you reflect on it, learn from it, and move on from it as quickly as possible. Now, focus your energy on getting the next soap role ASAP. You have experience behind you now. If you have not been written out of a Soap for creative reasons or been unceremoniously fired, then there is the classic mistake: you have decided to take yourself out of the show. This tends to happen when your ego gets too large, you begin thinking you are now "big time" and don't need to work on a soap anymore. It can be a "heady" experience when you are instantaneously recognized in public, and if it has indeed gone to your head, you are in trouble.

There is nothing wrong, of course, with enjoying your new-found fame on a Soap, if you are choosing to *stay* with that Soap, but it is quite another thing should you be setting your sights elsewhere. Many, famous television and movie stars began their careers on Soaps, and this is a well recognized fact. You should not go into a Daytime Drama acting job thinking, however, that it is a springboard into making you a movie star. If you have, then I would be very careful. This is the exception, NOT the rule for most Soap actors. If such acting opportunities should present themselves, you are very, very lucky indeed. I've known many an actor who left Daytime to pursue another acting job that was "bigger and higher paying," and then came crawling back to their former show begging for their steady gig back. When those nice regular paychecks stop rolling in and you have lost the other acting gig, or worse, you ended up not getting it after all, it can get pretty bleak, pretty fast. "Don't quit your day job" is an age-old show business saying. It is told to actors/performers when they first start out, and it is as true today as the day it was first uttered. A Soap is your "day job." If you are lucky enough to get on one, and stay on one, count your blessings! Don't fool around with a good thing when you are suddenly "famous," because as they always say in Hollywood: "You can never become 'UN-famous'." Remember, you can lose your daytime television job just as fast as you landed it. This is a steady job with steady pay that most actors would give their eyeteeth to have. Do your job, show up on time, and deliver your lines as the writers have written them... no more, no less.

CHAPTER ELEVEN
Soap Opera Make-up

One afternoon in Los Angeles, when my daughter was around six years old, I went to pick up some scripts from the studio. When we walked inside the doors there was a Soap star greeting some visitor friends in the lobby. My little girl had grown up watching Soaps, because it was my work and she knew some of my closest friends were Soap stars. Still, she had never seen any of them on-set in their full Soap make-up. As soon as the doors to the studio closed behind us, she remarked quite loudly (as children are wont to do): "Mommy, they wear soooo much MAKE-UP!"

Yes, it is true, Soap Opera actors have to wear a tremendous amount of make-up. Those Extreme Close-Ups (ECUs) are brutal and you have to wear enough make-up so you are what I call "bullet proof." Soap Operas are shot on tape and not film, and tape is mercilessly unforgiving! When your limbs are exposed, there is body make-up applied; when there are any torso shots or upper body shots, body make-up is applied; when there are bathing suit shots, body make-up is applied; and when you are doing love scenes in bed, body make-up is applied. Basically, when any area of skin is exposed, make-up is applied. When the hands are exposed and make-up hasn't been applied to them it is glaringly obvious. I used to be a make-up artist, so I notice these details, as do many loyal viewers.

Primetime TV, Cable, and the Internet are all shot on film so there is a graininess to it that allows for a little less make-up. You have to wear a significant amount of make-up on television, because the lighting on TV is so harsh. On film, it is even yet another "generation" removed from tape. Primetime TV, Cable and Internet are still another generation removed from tape, and film is yet another. It is a well-known show business fact that the famous Oscar Award-winning actor, Spencer Tracy, never wore make-up in any of his motion pictures; he simply didn't see the need for it. This would not have been possible had he starred in a Daytime Drama. With the super "hot" lights used in Daytime, and the fact that they are all on tape, Tracy's rugged and handsome appearance would have looked bizarre and out of place. There is no getting around the need for bulletproof make-up on Soaps!

CHAPTER TWELVE

The 3-Camera Shoot

My father, Robert H. Forward, pioneered the use of the 3-camera shoot for television in the early 1950s. I was always on TV and film sound stages as a child growing up. When my Soap Opera directorial mentor, the four-time consecutive Daytime Emmy Award-winning director for *The Young and the Restless*, Rudy Vejar, took me under his wing and taught me both how to act in front of the camera, and how to direct behind the camera...it was magic. I had the opportunity to perform in front of the camera, be in the director's booth, and watch how a Soap is directed. Rudy drummed into me that the first rule of Soap Opera acting is never turn your back to the camera unless you are directed to do so.

On Soap Opera sets there are only three physical walls and the three cameras are where the fourth wall would be. In all forms of acting there is never a fourth wall; not in the theater, not in Daytime, Primetime, or Cable. It is your job is to build the fourth wall. In the theater, an actor plays "out" to the audience—the audience is your fourth wall. In the case of Soap Operas your three cameras are where a live audience would be. Soap rules to live by on the set: you never look straight into the camera and you never turn your back to it.

In the director's booth, with all those huge monitors mounted on the wall, Rudy looked intently at each of them as he snapped his fingers and commanded in every conceivable order: "Camera 1 (SNAP), Camera 3 (SNAP), Camera 2 (SNAP!). Camera 3 (SNAP!), Camera 1(SNAP!), Camera 2 (SNAP!). Camera 2 (SNAP!), Camera 3 (SNAP!), Camera 1 (SNAP!)." And so on and so on in no particular order. I watched how smoothly the three camera operators, with their headsets always on, worked each of their cameras with incredible precision as Rudy commanded them in seemingly random order. The director makes all those decisions. And you thought only the actors had it tough!

Watching a truly fine Soap Opera director work is quite an honor. There are usually three or four directors on a Soap, depending on the length of that particular show. Each director directs one episode. They must bring continuity to the show as well as diversity so that the show always stays fresh. Certain directors are better at certain types of episodes than others and that is what keeps it so challenging to direct Soap Operas.

At this point it is important to explain about Soaps that shoot "in sequence," and those that shoot "out of sequence." A Soap that shoots in sequence is when one day's script is shot in its entirety in one day. All the scenes in that one script are shot that same day. A Soap that shoots out of sequence is one where up to four days of scripts are shot in one day and the same actors are not in all of the various scenes being shot. Of course there are times when certain scenes are shot "post- tape" and "pre-tape," as the script dictates.

You now probably realize just how much work goes into a Soap Opera in front of the cameras, behind the scenes, and how much mutual trust and respect is needed to pull off terrific, cohesive teamwork.

Not everyone can direct. There are good directors and there are bad ones. I remember one of many times I was on a particular Soap set, and the director was such a tyrant that the actors had a very rough time getting their shots and scenes in on time. Soap directors, and directors in general, have a very tough job, but no actor likes being shouted at to get a performance, and in fact, it can delay performances because the actors, no matter how seasoned, become rattled. Every actor I knew on that Soap hated that director and dreaded the days they had to shoot with him. The reason the Soap never got rid of him was he brought exactly what they wanted to the episodes he directed. I also remember a director on a major motion picture that was shot in my family home back in the 1960s. In major motion pictures you only have one director throughout the entire film. This incident took place at the end of the film while it was being shot entirely at my house—interiors and exteriors. It featured two very famous actors in the leads and the director was a tyrant. One evening, they were shooting an interior scene and I could hear that director screaming every direction at the actors. I came out to watch and one of the actors (the more famous of the two) got up from the furniture on the set, went over to the director on his dolly, and told him never to speak to him that way again or he was going to quit right then and there. With millions and millions of dollars at stake this far along in the picture that director got the message!

In films, the director is right there, on set with the actors, but in Soaps they are in the director's booth with an intercom system and cannot be disturbed. My point in telling you these two stories is simply to point out that any director who thinks that yelling at an actor is the only way to guarantee a good performance out of them is dead wrong; it is nothing more than on-set bullying.

Your "call times" on a Soap are very specific. If you are on an hour-long show, everyone must call the day before for any script changes. If you are scheduled for a morning call time, you get to the studio by 6:30 AM to go through blocking and to rehearse and then you go to make-up and get into wardrobe. If you are part of the afternoon shooting schedule, you get to the studio by 11:00 AM and so go through the same routine. For a half-hour show you call in by 6:00 AM the day before for any script changes, get to the studio by 9:30 for an hour and a half rehearsal, break for an hour for lunch, and then tape. Of course you can come to the studio any time you like, provided you are not sharing a dressing room! As you can see, the pressure is on you to have your scenes shot on time, so the other actors can get theirs done. Some Soaps shoot their shows in one take and others give you the luxury of three takes. Regardless, it saves everybody time if you know your lines and can finish your scenes promptly.

A Soap actor friend of mine used to become very frustrated with a particular new actor who was hired to play opposite him. This new actor was used to Primetime and movies and she was quite the diva. She felt that she should be indulged with her takes, because she was, after all, a "pro." She would stop a scene without hearing "CUT!" from the director, because she felt she could do it better with another take. This went on take after take after take... same excuse with each take. Breathtaking gall; possibly the worst thing any actor can do. Everyone went crazy with this diva because she held up production every day she shot! Needless to say, she didn't last long.

Each director is responsible for maintaining the continuity and the tone of the script as the writers have written it. Again, this reinforces just how much of an ensemble and collaborative effort a Soap Opera really is. The use of different directors is what keeps a Soap fresh and gives each Soap Opera its own unique "pop and sizzle."

Chapter Thirteen

Kissing Scenes, Chemistry, and Crying

I spoke about pop and sizzle in the previous chapter and that is the perfect segue to this chapter about kissing scenes. Some of you will be thrown into them immediately, perhaps on your very first day of shooting. It is all dictated by your storyline. For others of you, it will take some time, but at some point in the developing storyline of your character it will happen. When it does, you need to be ready. For the most part, it is very unromantic because of the strict blocking required to do love scenes on a Soap. It is very specific and technical. Simulated sex in bed scenes requires very specific body movements for both scene partners because you have three cameras. Nobody is naked and the bed sheets are strategically attached to your bodies with an adhesive to prevent slippage or the sheets from sliding all over the place. Sometimes a bathing suit-type wardrobe is made for you out of the same material as the sheets... it's up to the wardrobe department.

Chemistry can, and does, quite naturally develop between scene partners in romantic scenes. In order to play the scenes as your character is written and play them passionately as the script dictates, sometimes the lines can get blurred. No matter how good an actor you are, it sometimes just can't be helped. How you handle it is what matters. I know a number of Soap actors who have ended up getting into "on set" relationships with their co-stars, no matter how unintentionally. I remember visiting a friend on a Soap one day in his dressing room; I was helping him to run lines and in walked two of his co-stars, who were romantically involved with each other on the show. After a quick meet and greet, I was completely shocked when they started climbing all over each other when they thought we weren't looking. I knew one of them was married and the other was single and dating. I learned something that day; what goes on at the studio, stays at the studio. The choice, as an actor, is yours. What you choose to do, or choose not to do, is between you and your co-star. As long as your personal life doesn't cross over into your professional life or visa-versa, nobody cares. If it does... well... there could be painful repercussions, both personally and professionally.

Another type of a challenge in intimate scenes is crying. Being required to cry on cue is a big part of Soap Opera acting. Some actors can easily cry on cue and others cannot. In the case of the latter, eye drops are provided, the actor puts them in and the scene continues to be shot. Crying scenes are equally difficult whether you are acting alone or with a scene partner. They require you to draw your audience into your hardship, pain, and sorrow.

DÉNOUEMENT

The two questions I am asked most frequently are:

1. Why did you choose to teach Soap Opera acting? My answer is: I grew up in both an entertainment and a high society family. In my home there was a TV set in every room. The TVs in my home were never on in the daytime, because my mother never watched Daytime television and my father worked in Primetime. As a result, I never watched an American Soap Opera as a child. We had a live-in Mexican maid, though, and she watched her Telenovelas religiously, so I couldn't help but catch one or two of them on occasion! I watched my first American Soap Opera in the early 1980s. I immediately found the writing superb, the quality of acting very impressive, and the camera techniques amazing. I have never stopped watching them from that day to this!

2. Does Soap Opera acting differ from any other form of acting? My answer is a resounding YES! The timing, the dramatic slow speed, the cadence, the speech modulation, the intensity in the eyes and the body language...all of it is its own singular genre, absolutely no doubt about it! When I was first starting out teaching Soap Opera acting, a very famous Soap actor asked me why I thought Soap Opera acting was different from any other type of acting. He told me he saw no difference in acting styles at all. I asked one of his fellow cast members why that actor would have said what he said, and that cast member laughed heartily, and remarked: "Of course he would see no difference; he is the 'KING OF SLOW'!!"

I think Soap Opera actors are, without a doubt, some of the finest and most hard-working actors in the world, because their commitment to the work and to their characters is extraordinary; the pace and the scope of the work are unparalleled in the world of acting. Few actors are capable of sustaining this level of commitment to an ever-changing storyline for years, much less decades.

Over the decades, Soap Operas have become iconic touchstones in our society and culture. They tap into all of our human emotions; love, loss, betrayal, triumph, vengeance, happiness, and despair, all through the evolving lives of the fascinating characters the writers have created. Just from having read my book, you have probably learned a little something more about acting in the rich world of Soap Operas, and how the intertwining lives of the characters, and their deep storylines have captivated audiences for generations.

For others of you perhaps this has been a learning experience of a different kind. I hope this has helped clarify whether this is the direction you want your acting career to go in. Regardless of what you choose, I sincerely hope you have enjoyed reading this book as much as I have enjoyed writing it. My greatest wish for all of you who aspire to work in this amazingly complex and rewarding acting field, and to those of you who are just curious about Soap Operas, is that you have come away a little smarter and wiser for having read it, and maybe, just maybe, you have learned a little something about yourselves in the process.

Whether you choose a brilliant career in Soap Opera that spans decades or you enjoy a half hour or an hour daily watching them, I wish you all the very best of luck wherever your dreams may take you. May you always have romance in your life and may you always embrace your life with as much drama, passion, and excitement as these characters.

So it is, in typical Soap Opera fashion, that I leave you with a very fond and grateful kiss.

NOTES

TABLE 1.2
NATURE OF FATIGUE

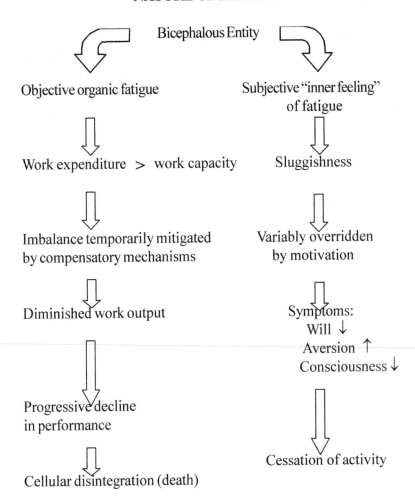

Bicephalous Entity

Objective organic fatigue

Subjective "inner feeling" of fatigue

Work expenditure > work capacity

Sluggishness

Imbalance temporarily mitigated by compensatory mechanisms

Variably overridden by motivation

Diminished work output

Symptoms:
Will ↓
Aversion ↑
Consciousness ↓

Progressive decline in performance

Cessation of activity

Cellular disintegration (death)

Fortunately we have a central nervous system endowed with self-awareness, fully able to respond to fatigue. The inner sensation of fatigue will give rise to unpleasant symptoms (tiredness, weariness, nausea, "psychic pain") and generate a decrease in the will to continue, a dampening of enthusiasm to a frank aversion and will dim somewhat the lights of consciousness. The end-result is cessation of activity. Biologically, this is important as it provides a breaking effect on activities that overtax the natural capacity of an organ. In this light, fatigue can be construed as a defense mechanism and a regulator of the equilibrium between work demand and work supply.

What is particularly interesting in this area of human biology is the inseparability of organic performance and psychological factors. The interactions are bidirectional and of great practical significance when strategies to manage fatigue are devised. Fatigue is indeed a bicephalous entity, not an irritating inconvenience flowing from frustrated physiology but a critically important element in the regulatory structures of the human body.

STATES FREQUENTLY CONFUSED WITH FATIGUE

Being an ill-defined sensation itself and there being many different, poorly-differentiated inner sensations in the human body, fatigue is easily confused with them and, occasionally, indistinguishable.

- ■ Frustration is often referred to as being "tired" of something. When a parent is "tired" of his child's behavior, it denotes more a feeling of irritated exasperation than actual fatigue (although it may result in fatigue).
- ■ Boredom lends a semblance to fatigue but the apathy of dull monotony is different from the apathy of weariness. You can be bored silly and still be highly energetic.
- ■ Sleepiness is a common aftermath of fatigue, but sleepiness can be induced by other physiologic states such as inactivity, uninteresting reading or TV viewing, just plain boredom and, most of all, a state of depression.

12